6 MINUTE SMARTS

COACH YOURSELF
BETTER, FAST

FIND YOUR CONFIDENCE

I0165093

Based on *Coach Yourself Confident* by Julie Smith

First published in Great Britain by Practical Inspiration Publishing, 2025

© Julie Smith and Practical Inspiration Publishing, 2025

The moral rights of the author have been asserted.

ISBN   978-1-78860-809-1   (paperback)
       978-1-78860-810-7   (ebook)

All rights reserved. This book, or any portion thereof, may not be reproduced without the express written permission of the publisher.

Every effort has been made to trace copyright holders and to obtain their permission for the use of copyright material. The publisher apologizes for any errors or omissions and would be grateful if notified of any corrections that should be incorporated in future reprints or editions of this book.

EU GPSR representative: LOGOS EUROPE, 9 rue Nicolas Poussin, LA ROCHELLE 17000, France Contact@logoseurope.eu.

Want to bulk-buy copies of this book for your team and colleagues? We can customize the content and co-brand *Find Your Confidence* to suit your business's needs.

Please email info@practicalinspiration.com for more details.

Practical Inspiration
Publishing™

Contents

Series introduction

Welcome to *6-Minute Smarts!*

This is a series of very short books with one simple purpose: to introduce you to ideas that can make life and work better, and to give you time and space to think about how those ideas might apply to *your* life and work.

Each book introduces you to ten powerful ideas, but ideas on their own are useless – that's why each idea is followed by self-coaching questions to help you work out the 'so what?' for you in just six minutes of exploratory writing. What's exploratory writing? It's the kind of writing you do just for yourself, fast and free, without worrying what anyone else thinks. It's not just about getting ideas out of your head and onto paper where you can see them; it's about finding new connections and insights as you write. This is where the magic happens.

Whatever you're facing, there's a *6-Minute Smarts* book just for you. And once you've learned how to coach yourself through a new idea, you'll be smarter for life.

Find out more...

Introduction

I imagine that you picked up this book because you'd like to be more confident. You're not alone. As a coach, I know just how widespread this desire is. Confidence is a topic that comes up time and again – sometimes explicitly, sometimes hidden beneath concerns about leadership, influence or impact. In many cases, we uncover the impact of a harsh inner critic, a fear of failure or a quiet, persistent feeling of not being good enough.

I'd like to be more confident too. While I've managed to drastically diminish the self-doubt that plagued me during the early part of my career, I still allow it to undermine me at times. As my confidence has grown, so has my ambition. With each new challenge, I face fresh opportunities to quieten the voice of self-doubt. Confidence is work that is never complete.

I've written this book because I've seen the difference confidence makes – by its presence and by its absence. I want to share what I've learned through three decades of supporting others, in the hope that it will support you too.

We'll explore stories drawn from real coaching conversations, reflection prompts to help you understand your own confidence and simple practices that support growth. These tools are not a 'ten steps to confidence' formula. Confidence is personal. What works for one person may not work for another. But with awareness and conscious practice, you *can* find your own path.

So, what is confidence?

The word confidence comes from the Latin *confidere*, meaning 'to have full trust'. It's a quiet, steady feeling of 'I've got this'. Not the belief that you're infallible or gifted with superpowers, but the trust that whatever happens, you'll be OK. That you'll find a way through.

It's not about winning. It's not about attaching your worth to success (or failure). Glennon Doyle writes that true confidence is *loyalty to self*.[1] It means self-acceptance: 'This is me, imperfect and flawed, brilliant and unique.' Confidence allows you to resist the urge to mould yourself into a shape that will please others. It allows you to stand firm, to speak out, to take risks – not recklessly, but with calm self-trust.

Confidence shows up in specific moments, and it's an ongoing relationship with yourself. It comes and goes, and sometimes crashes. That's normal.

My aim is to help you build a particular kind of confidence – one I call *humble confidence*. An objective and compassionate view of yourself, humble confidence rests on the mantra: *I am good enough and I can be better*. It's based on the belief that we are already enough, and that growth comes from curiosity, not from trying to prove our worth.

How this book will support you

This book is structured as ten days of focused work. Each day explores one facet of confidence: the hidden cost of self-doubt, the voice of your inner critic, the language you use, the impact of comparison and more. You'll uncover what holds you back and build practical tools for stepping forward.

Confidence isn't a destination – it's a way of being in a relationship with yourself. It's not about eliminating self-doubt but resizing it. When your confidence aligns with your capability, you unlock momentum – and that momentum can change everything.

Let's get started.

Day 1

Setting your confidence aspiration

We all have confidence. Without it, we'd struggle to meet the world on a daily basis. You might not have the deep well of confidence to which you aspire. You might be more intimately acquainted with your self-doubt than you are with your confidence. But your confidence is there. My hope is that reading this book will enable you to better acquaint yourself with your confidence, to find ways to access more easily what one of my interviewees described as 'feeling powerful from the inside', and to grow a fuller, more robust sense of what you're capable of.

We're beginning by exploring what confidence gives us – as a way to solidify your intention to strengthen your self-trust. And in today's coaching questions, I'll be inviting you to get clear on your confidence goal.

Better odds

Confidence does not guarantee success, but it does stack the odds in your favour. There is truth in the words of Roman poet Virgil: *Possunt quia posse videntur* ('They can because they think they can'). Our confidence is self-fulfilling: believing that we can do something increases the chances of success.

The correlation between confidence and performance is evident in sport. Olympic hockey captain Kate Richardson-Walsh told me confidence was 'the thing', saying, 'the people who had an ability to maintain their confidence for longer or were able to get through the low confidence bits, those were the people who tended to be consistently performing at the top.' Tim Gallwey's book *The Inner Game of Tennis* puts it plainly: *Performance = potential − interference.*[2] Quietening the voices of self-doubt and self-condemnation allows us to draw fully on our abilities.

A willingness to say YES

When we're faced with the opportunity to do something new, we have no way of knowing whether or not we can do it unless we say yes. Saying yes allows us to stretch ourselves, and confidence makes it easier to do that.

Miranda Mapleton, a successful marketing leader, was asked to set up a brand-new charity which would use technology to empower patients and improve health. She wasn't a doctor, a technologist or a charity leader. But she said yes. 'Confidence came from knowing I'd done other things,' she told me. 'I know I can think. I've got a good brain here. I can do these different things I haven't done before.' Her confidence wasn't about having all the answers – it was about trusting that she could figure it out.

You might reflect on what's become possible for you when you've taken a deep breath and said yes. Confidence enables us to say yes to the full panoply of wonder, excitement, horror, uncertainty and fabulous craziness that life has to offer.

The trust of others

Confidence doesn't just influence our own performance – it affects how others perceive us. We often confuse confidence with competence. We trust the confident doctor, the self-assured speaker, the unflustered leader. Si Bradley, a former British Army colonel, put it this way in my research conversation with him: 'Within two minutes of meeting someone, I've thought to myself, I don't even know what you're going to ask me to do, but I'm going to do it because I have confidence in your ability.'

Confidence contagion

Confidence can spark a collective power. Kate Richardson-Walsh told me about her team's preparation for the Olympics: they each identified and shared their 'super strengths', creating a powerful sense of belief within the team. She described it as 'a steely knowledge' that whatever happened, they'd find a way to win. And they did, taking gold.

Confidence contagion works in business too. Ben Lamont, a senior HR Director, told me he's often found himself saying, 'I haven't got a clue how we're going to do this, but I know it can be done, and I know we'll find a way.' His belief becomes the team's belief.

So what? Over to you...

1. Think back to a moment when you were at your most confident. What physical sensations were you aware of? What emotions were present? What thoughts were running through your mind?

2. Continuing to reflect on the moment that came to mind in question 1, what did that confidence enable?

3. What is your aspiration in relation to confidence? What is the shift that you'd like to make? What would be different for you, and how would that feel? What would others see?

Day 2
Counting the cost of self-doubt

How does self-doubt show up for you? You may experience it as a constant second-guessing. You may struggle to own your strengths or take full credit for success. You may feel physically agitated – butterflies, tension, unease. It's possible that you hear it in your everyday speech – quiet tone, caveats, over-apologizing – these all convey a lack of trust in ourselves. We'll explore the language of confidence in more depth on Day 7.

The self-doubt tax

While self-doubt is a normal, unavoidable and in some ways useful part of the human experience, an excess of self-doubt is a heavy weight to carry. The 'self-doubt tax' is the name I give to the cost of giving too much power to our self-doubt. The tax is levied in two ways.

When we allow a lack of confidence to hold us back, we stay small and safe, paying the self-doubt tax in the form of missed opportunities. When we push ourselves to achieve impressive results despite a nagging self-doubt, we pay the tax in the form of overwork.

The dictionary tells us that a tax is 'a compulsory contribution to state revenue, levied by the government'. The thing about the self-doubt tax is that it's *voluntary*. If your self-doubt is over-sized, then a payment is due – but if you resize it, you can lower your tax bill.

Paying the tax in missed opportunities

Self-doubt can slow us down. At its worst, it can keep us at a standstill. In the grip of self-doubt, we seek to keep ourselves safe by holding back.

Ian Robertson puts it clearly in *How Confidence Works*:

> 'Fear means that you feel threatened, and when you feel unsafe, the only real alternatives are fight and flight... If the threat seems to come

from inside you, there's nothing to fight. So flight becomes the only option, and the safe and familiar your only refuge.'[3]

Sticking with the safe and familiar is understandable. It's comfortable and it can feel like the only sensible path, but it means that we miss out on opportunities, big and small.

One way of holding back is to stay quiet. In my work as a coach, I've met people who have deep insight, strong instincts and valuable ideas – but who rarely share them. They assume their thoughts must be obvious or irrelevant. Or they believe that unless what they say is perfect, it isn't worth saying at all.

My client Oliver was a striking example. Despite his expertise, he struggled to speak up in meetings. His internal bar was impossibly high. Unless his comment was original, succinct and flawlessly articulated, he kept it to himself. That ruled out 95% of what he might have contributed.

Oliver wasn't withdrawn or disengaged – quite the opposite. He was thoughtful and committed. But his self-doubt had formed a private rulebook that shut down his voice. That silence came at a cost: to his influence, his confidence and the team's access to his thinking.

A people leader in a major UK retailer told me she'd seen a similar pattern with graduate trainees:

'I'm just the grad – nobody's going to want to listen to me.' That thought led them to stay quiet. Staying quiet led them to believe they had nothing valuable to say. And so the cycle continued.

From missed moments to unfulfilled potential

When we stay small, we don't just miss one opportunity – we accumulate lost ground. We forgo the experiences that would challenge, grow and shape us. We stay stuck in self-censorship. Staying small can go beyond staying quiet when we have smart thinking to offer or stepping back from projects that would get us noticed. It can curtail our career progression when it shows up as a decision not to put ourselves forward for a stretching new role, despite having the required qualifications and experience. The tax is paid not in pounds or dollars, but in confidence, progress and fulfilment.

Paying the tax in overwork

It's perfectly possible to be under-confident and wildly successful, but there's a cost. 'I have this irrational fear that I'm going to get fired. I know it's irrational, but it's still there – I can't get rid of it.' Orlagh moved between laughter and exasperation as she explored her hidden fear with me during a coaching session. Orlagh was (and still is) hugely successful in her career, and she was weighed down by an inner commentary of doubt – a commentary that led her to work punishing hours. Orlagh's self-doubt tax was payable in the currency of overwork and exhaustion.

I've met and worked with many people like Orlagh. Incredibly successful individuals whose success has partly been driven by their self-doubt. In order to lessen their anxiety, they have pushed themselves excessively hard. They set punishingly high standards for everything they do; they over-deliver on every objective; they over-invest in preparation time for every meeting. While there's no question that these habits have contributed to their stellar results and impressive career paths, the personal cost is high. This kind of excessive effort is quite simply exhausting and can be a recipe for burn-out.

The turning point: awareness

As we'll see in the next chapters, your self-doubt isn't the enemy. You don't need to banish it – just resize it. That starts with becoming aware of how and when it taxes you most. Today's self-coaching questions focus on awareness.

So what? Over to you...

1. How does self-doubt show up for you? What do you notice in yourself, and what might others see and hear?

2. In what ways do you pay the self-doubt tax – in missed opportunities, in overwork, in both ways?

3. What would become possible if you were to dramatically reduce your self-doubt tax payment?

Day 3
Cultivating humble confidence

When it comes to confidence, more is not always better. Our aim is not to build our confidence level ever higher, our aim is to build just the right amount. The Goldilocks approach to confidence. 'Just the right amount' is a level of confidence that matches our capability. With just the right amount of confidence, our sense of what we are capable of aligns with the reality of our skills and abilities. This is humble confidence: a solid and balanced sense of self, neither inflating egotism nor diminishing self-doubt.

The anatomy of humble confidence

Humble confidence is grounded confidence; grounded in reality and grounded in an objective perspective of our capability. If we're humble, we have the ability to accurately assess our success and we can be OK with our inevitable, ordinary, human limitations.

This is what humble confidence sounds like:

- My strengths are clear to me. I know what I'm good at.
- I know what I'm not so good at, and I'm OK with that.
- I know that I can add to my list of strengths through focus and effort.
- I have navigated some tricky situations and I've come out the other side.
- If need be, I can navigate adversity again.
- I can face the unknown with a sense that I'll find what's needed within myself.

These sentences are founded on 'I' – they are about my own knowledge of myself, rather than relying on how others see me. These are not mantras to recite, they are articulations of a felt experience. I am not seeking to convince anyone – either myself or others – of my abilities or my self-assurance, I'm simply noticing what is true for me.

Humble confidence isn't static. 'Just the right amount' of confidence is the level that matches our skills and abilities, so as we expand our capability we expand our confidence.

The humble confidence mantra

With humble confidence, we can own our strengths. And at the same time, we know that there will always be ways that we can grow and develop. *I'm good enough AND I can be better* is the mantra of humble confidence. This can be a settling and affirming phrase to hold in your mind.

The humble confidence mantra can help as you step into a new domain. The mantra acknowledges two fundamental truths. First, that your self-worth is not attached to your performance in this new domain – you are good enough simply because of who you are. Second, that you have the capacity to grow and develop. By definition, a beginner has scope to learn. This is not a deficiency, it's simply the reality; when you start something new, you're not immediately skilled and at ease, but you can grow your skill (and your sense of ease) through focus and practise. You're not good at this new thing yet, but you will improve in time.

An antidote to overwork

We can apply a version of the humble confidence mantra to the results that we deliver: what I've done is good enough and there's always room to improve. We take satisfaction from our achievements and feel proud of what we have accomplished. And at the same time, we are clear that more is possible. I've done a brilliant job this year and there are more opportunities to go after in the next 12 months. It's enough. And more is possible. This way of thinking can be an antidote to the habit of overwork that showed up as a form of the self-doubt tax.

So what? Over to you...

1. Reflect on 'I'm good enough' – what are the many skills and strengths that you bring to your work?

2. Reflect on 'and I can be better' – what are your development areas and how do you feel about them?

3. Reflect on 'good enough and can be better' in relation to the results that you deliver – is there an opportunity to appreciate what you've delivered (and take a breath!) before pushing for more?

Day 4
Seeing yourself clearly

With humble confidence, our confidence matches the reality of our skills and capabilities. For some of us, seeing the reality of what we bring is really difficult. In fact, our lack of confidence can stem from a distortion in the way that we see ourselves. Our strengths and achievements look smaller to us than they do to others, while our weaknesses are magnified in our minds.

It's possible that you've heard 'you should be more confident!' many times from a colleague or friend. They go on to list your myriad strengths, but you can't believe them because your calibration is faulty. You don't see your strengths and your achievements as others see them – they look smaller to you. Worse than that, your weaknesses and your 'haven't done yets' look much bigger to you than they look to those around you.

Today our focus is on how you might see yourself in a way that more closely matches what your supportive 'you should be more confident' friend is seeing.

Feedback through a filter

When we hear feedback, we hold it up against our self-image. If the feedback doesn't fit with how we see ourselves, with how we evaluate our own capabilities, then it's difficult for us to process it. If our confidence lags behind our capability, positive feedback bounces off, unprocessed and unabsorbed because we can't square it with how we see ourselves. We find ways to explain it away – 'they're just being kind; they don't really mean it' or 'they wouldn't say that if they had to work with me all the time!'

I see clients who have well-developed defences for positive feedback. They resist, discount and sidestep positive evaluations. In the words of one client: 'I don't absorb positive feedback, so I don't get a boost from that... but negative feedback? Well, I really hear that, and I can go into a tunnel of self-criticism.' The gates are closed tightly against positive feedback, but they are thrown wide open for any hint of negative feedback. The reason we hear negative feedback really loudly if we're lacking confidence is that it fits only too well with our harsh, part-formed self-image. We see ourselves as lacking, therefore any critical feedback chimes with our own view. We hear the feedback and accept it as true because it reinforces our own sense of what we lack.

Taking ownership of our strengths

If your calibration is faulty, you don't see the true extent of your strengths, which makes it impossible for you to own your strengths and tricky to fully utilize them. You may also look at your achievements in the same distorted way, minimizing them. *It was actually quite easy. Anyone could have done it. There was a lot of luck really. It was largely down to Kate.*

It may be that you quickly put achievements behind you, immediately turning your attention to the next big thing. It's difficult, even impossible, for you to pause and acknowledge what you have achieved and to absorb the success that could fuel confidence.

Consciously acknowledging and owning our strengths and achievements can help to bring them into more realistic focus.

Seeing yourself clearly

With my coaching clients, I sometimes notice that the process of taking ownership of their strengths is uncomfortable, as they battle with programming from their childhood such as *no one likes a show-off* or *real talent is quiet – if you're good, you don't need to blow your own trumpet*. If you notice a similar discomfort in yourself, these ways of thinking might help to alleviate it. They are useful thoughts when considering your strengths.

- I'm better able to access and use my strengths if I'm clear about what they are.
- I can be brilliant at something and still have room to improve.
- Acknowledging a strength does not trigger complacency.
- Acknowledging how good I am at one thing is not the same as claiming to be good at everything.
- Acknowledging a strength is a statement of truth, not boasting.

So what? Over to you...

1. Imagine you're in an interview for your dream role – what would you say when asked to share your top three strengths?

2. Bring to mind a recent piece of positive feedback and express it here in multiple different ways. (The aim is to see if you can get closer to (fully) believing the feedback.)

3. Write a glowing review of a recent work achievement for an (imaginary) internal newsletter. One rule: no regrets or critiques outside of three 'learnings for next time' at the end.

Day 5
Tackling your confidence saboteurs

If we are to grow a robust and enduring feeling of confidence, we need to understand our confidence saboteurs. We need to understand what can drain our self-belief at the very moment that we need it and what can erode confidence over time. All too often we unintentionally diminish our own confidence. Most of the saboteurs that we'll consider in this chapter have something in common – they exist in your own head. This means that you can take control. It's not easy, but it's possible to tackle the saboteurs and claim your confidence.

Comparisonitis

My own confidence took a blow when I found myself among an incredibly able group of students on my history degree course. One student in particular became the focus of my comparisonitis: Esme. Quick thinking, eloquent and willing to speak out, Esme seemed to me to be everything that I wasn't. Alongside her in a seminar group, I didn't think *what a fantastic person to learn from*. No. Instead I thought *I'm nowhere near as good as her*.

Our brains are wired to compare. It's how we evaluate our place in the world. But unmanaged, this habit becomes corrosive. It leads us to fixate on what we lack, rather than value what we bring.

The issue with comparisonitis is not how we see the other person. The issue is what our view of the other person does to the way that we see ourselves. You can dismantle comparisonitis and reset the way you see yourself by shifting from a 'less-than' or 'more-than' comparison to a complementary evaluation: in what ways do you and the other person have complementary skills? For example, *Satnam is so much more creative than me* might become *Satnam and I are good at thinking together. She generates lots of ideas and we work together to refine them and figure out how they could work in practice.*

FOPO

FOPO is the fear of other people's opinions. Most human beings are uncomfortable about being judged. After all, we're wired to care about what others think of us. For early humans, not caring about others' reactions might have led to being ostracized or banished from the tribe; a dangerous position. For self-doubt taxpayers, the discomfort is heightened because we're already overly alert to our shortcomings; we don't need additional critical voices. We really don't want (or need) other people to signpost our flaws, and our FOPO leads to us stepping back and avoiding the spotlight.

The false assumption behind FOPO is that it's possible to be viewed positively by everyone we come across. That if we try hard enough, we can ensure that everyone has a good opinion of us. If we can let go of this fantasy, it becomes easier to deal with critical feedback. Of course feedback is valuable, but it should be taken alongside your own opinions and feelings. We can care what other people think without fearing their judgement. Not everyone will like what we do. That's inevitable. And it's OK.

Mindreading

You are presenting and Bradley on the front row yawns theatrically and rubs his face with his hands. *Oh my God. He's absolutely bored to tears. Everyone else must feel the same.* The sabotage of confidence happens when you are convinced by your interpretation; when in that moment, you believe that you can read minds. It can feel like your certainty in yourself drops like a stone, an immediate response to what you think is someone's reaction.

Remember, unless someone tells you, there is no way that you can possibly know what is going through their mind. You can pick up clues, sure. But you need to accept that you might be right, you might be wrong. You don't have the ability to read minds.

So start simply by being aware that you (and me, and all of us) make up stories that aren't always true. Noticing and telling yourself 'I'm doing that mindreading thing again' might be enough to lessen the certainty that you attach to your interpretation. Perhaps Bradley on the front row is just tired. Perhaps he is trying to undermine you, or perhaps that's just how he yawns.

Second, you can ask the person to share what they're thinking instead of assuming that you know. You might not want to stop mid-presentation and demand to know why Bradley is yawning, but you could ask a more general check-in question of the audience: 'How's this working for you so far? Are you with me? Any requests of me at this point?' Scary? Yes. But this is an invitation for data that will be really useful to you, whatever form it takes. If the response is a resounding 'all good', then it will be easier to set aside your *Bradley-yawned-everyone-must-be-bored* story. If your invitation results in a request to do things differently, then you have the chance to make changes in the moment.

Overthinking

Overthinking is the mental equivalent of running on a treadmill: no forward movement, just exhaustion (only without the benefits of a physical workout).

Our mental running-on-the-spot is usually focused on the past or on the future; overthinking isn't about the here and now. We expend energy in worry and regret about what we've done (or haven't done) or said (or not said) in the past. We relive painful situations over and over again, giving ourselves ample opportunity to spot errors of judgement or missed chances.

When we get caught up in future-focused overthinking, we might be gripped by nerves, or we might be seeking ways to control what has not yet happened. We rehearse how a situation might play out, with the emphasis on drama, nervous anticipation, anxiety and fear.

Mindfulness practices can be an antidote to both kinds of overthinking because it brings our attention to the present moment – rather than stepping back into the past or forward into the future, our focus is on the here and now.

Perfectionism

High standards can be useful. They can fuel success at school, university and work. Perfectionism is high standards on steroids. It's an expectation of self that is unreasonable, unattainable.

The perfectionism saboteur crushes confidence because we've set up a gap – a gap between what we deliver (however brilliant it is) and the impossible bar of perfection. We don't see what we've done and appreciate the brilliance; we focus instead on what's not perfect.

I like author Seth Godin's definition of perfect: 'Perfect doesn't mean flawless. Perfect means it does exactly what I need it to do.' I think this offers us an antidote to perfectionism – a focus on what's really needed, or in other words, a focus on what's good enough.

When you embark on a piece of work, be clear on what you need it to do. What exactly is the goal? With this piece of work, what is good enough? I recognize that there will be times when you want to exceed 'good enough' on a particular piece of work. That's understandable, and it's OK *as long as you are making a conscious choice to do so*. We're not seeking to just lower our standards; we're seeking to use more precision in choosing how we invest our limited energies. The aim is to focus on the achievement of good enough, not on the impossibility of perfection.

So what? Over to you...

1. Which confidence saboteur do you most recognize in yourself?

2. In what ways has that saboteur shown up in your work life over the past seven days?

3. What's one tactic you can try to lessen its power this week?

Day 6
Uncovering your inner critic

Yesterday you might have spotted that there was something (or rather, someone) who was conspicuously absent in our consideration of confidence saboteurs. That's because they're the focus of today's chapter. Yes, today, we're giving our full attention to the inner critic.

One of the things that unites those of us who wish to increase our confidence is that our inner critic is particularly loud, not easily dissuaded and painfully present. It's the voice that watches, judges and whispers: *You're not good enough*. It disconnects us from the present, undermines our trust in ourselves and dulls our strengths.

The inner critic's intention isn't malicious. It's trying to be helpful – trying to keep us safe. It wants to protect us from getting it wrong, looking foolish or being rejected. But its vigilance is often out of proportion, and the safety it offers comes at the cost of growth, visibility and ease.

My own inner critic is incredibly hard-working. He – for me, it's a 'he' – is always on the lookout for signals that I've done something wrong or failed to meet a standard. For him, 'wrong' has a very wide definition. I know I'm not alone in this. From decades of coaching, I've seen how many high-functioning, capable people live with a persistent internal narrator who questions their every move.

How the inner critic shows up

The inner critic often speaks in a familiar, cutting tone. *You sound like an idiot. You should have known better. That wasn't good enough.* Its focus is narrow – it notices flaws, not progress; risks, not strengths.

Ironically, your inner critic may sound extremely confident. It doesn't hesitate. It delivers sweeping judgements with certainty. And if you dare to push past it, it's ready with *I told you so.*

Recognizing your inner critic's strategy

Your inner critic likely has a dominant tactic. Drawing on the work of Taibi Kahler,[4] here are five common strategies:

- *Be perfect* – sets impossibly high standards
- *Please others* – prioritizes external approval
- *Go faster* – urges relentless pace and productivity
- *Don't fail* – makes success the only option
- *Be strong* – discourages vulnerability or asking for help.

Many of us carry a blend. 'Be perfect' + 'please others' is especially draining, pushing us to meet standards that are not only high but also conflicting. We strive to be flawless while keeping everyone happy – and blame ourselves when that's not possible.

Unmasking the critic

The inner critic's power lies in its stealth. It feels like truth because it speaks from inside our heads. But it's not *us* – it's a voice we've absorbed and internalized over time. The first step to weakening it is to name it, see it and create distance from it.

Try giving your critic a name. (Mine's called Nigel.) Naming it underlines that it's not you – it's a part of you, but it's not in charge.

Draw your critic. Literally. What does it look like? A monster? A bossy teacher? A cartoon villain? The act of drawing it – no matter how silly – can be disarming.

Write down what your critic says. Transcribe the thoughts exactly. You may notice how exaggerated or irrational they are when seen on the page.

And finally, talk to it. Acknowledge its good intentions. Thank it for trying to look after you and explain the choice that you are making. *Thank you for trying to keep me safe – I hear that you think that speaking in this meeting is risky, but I'm choosing to share my point of view now...*

Fooling your critic

August Wilson, the playwright, used to write on paper napkins. When asked why, he said that if he pulled out a tablet, it meant he was 'writing' – and that made him self-conscious. But writing on napkins didn't trigger his inner critic. It felt informal, safe, unthreatening.[5]

What's your version of the paper napkin? Where can you start small, sketch roughly or act 'as if' it doesn't count – so you can slip past the critic's grip?

The power of noticing

The more often you notice your critic, the more power you gain. You don't need to argue with it, you just need to see it. And each time you respond with curiosity instead of compliance, you reclaim a little more space to move.

Today's self-coaching is intended to heighten the sensitivity of your inner critic antennae – so that you can more easily notice when they're getting in your way.

So what? Over to you...

1. Use the space below to draw (and name) your inner critic. *If your inner critic pops up with a point of view about your drawing skill, offer a polite 'thank you' and then keep drawing.*

2. What do you hear most often from your inner critic? Write down a couple of its favourite phrases and make a note of what was happening when you most recently heard them.

3. Over the coming week, what will you try in order to turn down the volume on your inner critic?

Day 7

Speaking the language of confidence

Language is very powerful. Language does
not just describe reality. Language creates the
reality it describes.

Desmond Tutu

The way we speak – to ourselves and to others –
shapes how we feel. It shapes how others see us. The
words we choose are not just descriptors; they are
creators of experience. This is why the language of
self-doubt deserves our attention.

Many of us use self-doubting language out of
habit. Phrases like 'It's probably a silly idea, but...'
or 'You've probably already thought of this...'
signal tentativeness before we've even said anything

substantive. These phrases may sound like politeness, but they can dilute our message and our sense of authority. They tell others – and ourselves – that we don't fully trust what we're saying. We are handing power to our inner critic by speaking their words aloud.

A common example is the phrase, 'Does that make sense?' While it might appear to be a question about clarity, it often reveals a deeper self-doubt: *Please can you assuage my doubt and reassure me that I have said something worthwhile?* More confident alternatives to experiment with include 'What do you make of that?', Do you have any questions so far?' and 'Any reflections on that?'

Minimizing and softening language

We often hedge our statements. Words like *just, maybe, perhaps, a little, I think, sort of* and *kind of* creep into our everyday vocabulary and weaken what we're trying to say. 'I just wanted to check...', 'I was kind of wondering...', 'Maybe we could possibly...' – these are all signals of shrinking back.

Such language is often used unconsciously, especially by those with a strong drive to be liked or not appear too assertive. But it has a real impact on how our ideas land and how we perceive our own authority. It undermines confidence – not only in others' eyes but in our own experience.

Try this: Open a few of your recent emails. Highlight every instance of *just, maybe, possibly* or *I think*. Then read the same message aloud with those words removed. What changes? Does your message feel more confident? Does it still feel like you?

Over-apologizing: a reflex of self-doubt

Apologizing unnecessarily is a common verbal habit that signals self-doubt. You might hear yourself say, 'Sorry, I should've made that clearer,' or 'Apologies, I'm rambling.' You might preface disagreement with 'Sorry, but I see it differently.'

In these moments, you're asking for forgiveness before you've done anything wrong. You're assuming that speaking your mind or taking up space is something to be excused. But expressing an idea, asking a question or offering a different view is not something you need to apologize for.

One useful awareness tool is to keep a 'sorry tally' – a count of how often you say sorry in a single day. You might also ask a colleague to observe and reflect back what they hear – if it's an automatic habit, you might not notice you're doing it. If it seems like a high tally of unnecessary apologies, experiment with a 'no sorry meeting' or a 'no sorry day' to see if you can interrupt the urge to apologize.

This isn't about erasing politeness or humility. It's about noticing when 'sorry' is really a placeholder for self-doubt.

Self-deprecating humour

Self-doubt also shows up in our humour. Jokes like 'My brain's mush today', or 'Ha! Typical me, always messing things up,' can seem harmless. They might even make us feel relatable. But over time, these repeated statements create a self-image that is difficult to shake. They invite others to join in the doubt, even if unintentionally.

These jokes are often rooted in a desire to appear modest, to signal that we're not taking ourselves too seriously. But if the cost is that others take us *less* seriously – or that we reinforce our own inner critic – it may not be worth it.

Try this: Keep a log of your self-deprecating remarks over the course of a week. Then read them back. Do they still seem funny? Are they really jokes – or a shield? What might be true underneath the humour?

Language and presence

It's not just *what* we say. It's *how* we say it. Tone, tempo and emphasis can all signal confidence – or uncertainty. A quiet, hesitant tone makes even a strong idea sound weak. A rushed pace can give the impression of nervousness or lack of conviction.

In coaching, I've often worked with clients on finding a steady, grounded speaking style – one that reflects the calm self-trust they're trying to build. Slowing down, pausing and owning your space can be subtle but powerful shifts.

Confidence is contagious, as we saw earlier. And it starts in the words and tone we choose. The more you speak from a place of centred clarity, the more others will mirror that belief back to you.

The ripple effect of language

Changing your language habits can feel awkward at first. You may worry about sounding too blunt or not like yourself. But confidence and authenticity are not opposites. You can speak with warmth and still sound grounded. You can challenge someone and still be respectful. You can ask for support without apology.

Awareness is the starting point. Once you begin to notice your default patterns, you gain the power to choose. And with each small shift – removing a softener, holding your pause, stating your idea cleanly – you build the muscle of humble confidence.

So what? Over to you...

1. What phrase or verbal habit do you use that might be shrinking your message?

2. In what situations do you most notice yourself softening or apologizing – and what might be behind it?

3. What's one experiment you could run this week to speak with a little less self-doubt?

Day 8

Surviving dips and setbacks

Our sense of confidence, the extent to which we trust ourselves, ebbs and flows over time. No one feels confident all the time. Even the most experienced leaders have moments when their self-trust wavers. A failed project, a tough piece of feedback, a health issue – any of these can cause a dip. The difference isn't whether you experience the drop. It's how you respond.

The confidence line graph

If I were to plot my confidence over time on a line graph where the vertical axis represents my level of confidence and the horizontal axis represents time, it wouldn't be a neat straight line. The overall trend is upwards, but it's really scratchy in places. There are some big gains, a few big drops and a lot of little ups and downs, the accumulation of which is a significantly higher level of confidence now than the level I enjoyed 10, 20, 30 years ago.

Your confidence line graph would look different to mine, but I suspect it too would be wobbly. Your wobbles might be big or small, frequent or infrequent, but they would be there. But just like any graph, what matters is not a single data point but the overall trajectory.

What's helpful is to observe your graph with curiosity. Where are the peaks? Where are the troughs? What triggers each? The more you understand your own pattern, the more you can learn to navigate it.

The inevitability of setbacks

Setbacks are part of the journey – not a detour from it. But when they happen, they can shake us. We may question our capability. We may assume the dip means we've 'lost' our confidence altogether.

As one client put it: 'You spend years building up confidence and then it disappears in a puff of smoke.'

Drops in confidence are not always as dramatic as this, but ups and downs are unavoidable and we need to develop ways to minimize the dips. It's inevitable that plans will go awry, hiccups will happen, mistakes will be made. If we're not careful, this kind of day-to-day setback can trigger a painful confidence dip that leaves us trapped in our self-doubt, reluctant to step forward and take action again.

The power of perspective

So how can we avoid a day-to-day setback becoming a painful confidence dip? The first thing to acknowledge is that it's human to feel disappointed, embarrassed, frustrated when something doesn't go as we'd hoped. These feelings are normal and natural, and it's possible that they might pass within a matter of hours. What turns a setback into a confidence dip is when our inner critic gets involved and adds a self-kicking into the emotional swirl. *I worked really hard on putting the deal together, but it didn't go through* becomes *I really messed it up, I should have anticipated all of their objections* becomes *I'm just not commercial enough.* What started as a setback becomes a large dose of self-doubt. We can interrupt this process by putting what happened into perspective.

Step 1: remind yourself just how boringly normal it is. Setbacks aren't pleasant, but they are part of being human so there's no need to go hunting for the particular personal deficit that caused this thing to happen to you. It happened and now you have a choice about how you respond to that fact.

Step 2: see the grey. Most situations aren't wholly good or wholly bad. A simple way to keep the setback in perspective is to look for the grey. *My project proposal didn't get signed off, but I learned more about what is important to the executive team. I didn't get the role that I went for, but there was some encouraging feedback from the hiring manager.*

Step 3: mentally step forward in time. Try stepping into the future and looking at the setback from the perspective of a week, a month, a year's time. How significant does it look from there? Mental time travel offers a way to see the setback for what it is: a tricky episode in a much longer story, not a moment that defines who you are or what you're capable of.

Take the bounce

It might sound counterintuitive, but a confidence dip can sometimes trigger a confidence gain. Perhaps you surprise yourself with your ability to get through a tricky situation. Things don't go as expected, but you keep on going, you find another way. If you use this as a trigger to recalibrate your sense of self, then you can expand your understanding of what you're capable of and fuel your confidence.

Fellow coach Andy Brett puts it beautifully: 'Confidence is the quiet, steady feeling of "I've got this" that (for me) comes with the knowledge that I've screwed-up in pretty much every way possible at some point in the past and recovered each time.' Acknowledging that you've had setbacks and you've overcome them is empowering: *I messed up a, b, c, d, e, f... and I'm still OK, so I can take on whatever comes next.*

What Andy is talking about here is the way that our experiences can contribute to a growing feeling of internal confidence. This is the theme – growing confidence from within – that we'll be digging into tomorrow.

So what? Over to you...

1. Try drawing your own confidence line graph – what patterns do you notice?

2. Identify a setback you've experienced in the last six months. Write down how you experienced the setback at the time. Write down how you see it now. Compare and contrast – what do you notice?

3. Write a list of times when you've surprised yourself – perhaps you got through something tricky, stepped up to a new challenge, recovered from a setback. What strikes you as you read your list?

Day 9

Growing confidence
from within

The most robust version of confidence is grown from within. There is a solidity to this homegrown confidence, a solidity that brings to mind Maya Angelou's words: 'Nothing can dim the light which shines from within.'

Of course, boosts to your confidence often spring from external sources: a job title that provides a label for your level of achievement, qualifications that signpost your knowledge, or the praise that you receive from others. These boosts can make a difference to the way that you feel about yourself, triggering pride and swelling your confidence. But there's a risk of this being a temporary impact. If you don't internalize these reasons to be confident, then the lift in confidence is fleeting.

The fragility of borrowed confidence

If we're relying on others for validation, then it builds our confidence when we hear positive things, but confidence can crash when they criticize. We have invested power in their opinion; good when the opinion is a positive one, potentially disastrously undermining when it isn't. Our sense of our own ability is based on what they think. Our sense of self is only on loan to us and our confidence is only present for as long as the other person holds a positive evaluation of us. If that person is our boss and they change jobs, our confidence evaporates. If the cheerleaders from whom we borrow our confidence are within the organization where we work, what does that mean for our ability to choose to leave? Can we really risk leaving our sense of confidence behind, in the hands of our former colleagues?

It's not as straightforward as 'borrowing confidence = bad', however. Borrowed confidence is OK if it's a short-term loan. Borrowing confidence from a supportive leader can be a key step on the journey to generating a more solid, internal belief in your own capability. Believers can help us to find our confidence for ourselves, following the path that they set out through unstinting belief and encouragement.

This is the paradox of borrowed confidence: it can help us get started, but unless we consciously internalize it, it won't sustain us.

Keeping up with yourself

Sometimes we outgrow our own self-image. We evolve, but we forget to update our internal narrative.

When I interviewed Rebecca, she shared her experience of this. Rebecca had stepped up to Global Vice President, taken on new challenges and grown in capability – but her self-concept hadn't fully caught up. 'There's still a bit of me that feels like a graduate trainee who's trying to prove herself,' she told me. Rebecca's awareness serves her well – knowing that somewhere inside her is the graduate trainee with a fair degree of self-doubt and a need to prove herself means that she can spot the times when old patterns resurface and she can reset her confidence.

This isn't unusual. Our self-image often lags behind our actual development. We keep seeing ourselves as the junior, the beginner, the one who's still figuring it out – even when others see us as confident and competent. There's a gap between who we are and who we think we are.

Part of growing confidence from within is catching up with yourself. It's noticing the gap – and gently closing it. That might mean reflecting on feedback you've received, naming your progress or simply acknowledging the ways in which you've changed.

Permission to be you

One of the most significant things that you can do to grow your confidence from the inside is to give yourself full permission to be who you are. This means being clear about your values, being clear about the impact that you want to have on those around you, being clear on the impact you want to have in your organization or on wider society. This clarity comes from the inside – it's your own version of 'success', not shaped by the expectations of others, but creating your own version of what good looks like.

As part of my research on confidence I spoke to Michelle, head of an independent school. Inevitably those around her – teachers, students, parents, governors – all have their own mental model of a good headteacher, their own set of expectations. Michelle is attuned to this array of expectations – she has to be – but she is not constrained or overly influenced by them.

> 'When I first took on the role, it's as though I put on a cloak of headship which didn't really fit me – it was a cloak that represented the way I thought a headteacher should be. But as I grew into the role, I discarded the cloak, seeing that it wasn't needed. I now have the confidence to be the kind of headteacher that I am. I'm not going to be the remote, austere figure. I'm not like that. I'm like this.'

I think that's a wonderful example of the liberating power of giving yourself permission to be you.

This kind of confidence takes time to grow. But it's real — and it's yours.

So what? Over to you...

1. Who or what have you relied on for confidence in the past — and what might it look like to bring more of that trust inside?

2. Where in your life has your growth outpaced your self-image — and how could you update the story you tell yourself?

3. To what extent do you give yourself 'permission to be you' in the way that you do your current role?

Day 10
Sustaining confidence, sustaining growth

Finding your confidence is not a one-off activity. You'll have days when self-doubt creeps in again. You'll face new challenges that unsettle your footing. That doesn't mean you're back at square one – it means you're human.

The goal is not to eliminate doubt forever. It's to *stay in relationship* with your confidence – to tend to it, return to it and grow it with intention over time.

Long-term self-trust

Sustaining confidence over time isn't about feeling perpetually invincible. It's about developing a resilient sense of humble confidence that holds steady – even when life gets messy. Confidence that lasts is built on *self-trust*. It's not about surface-level assurance. It's the deeper knowing that you can handle what comes – that you have the resources, the resilience and the capacity to find your way through.

This kind of self-trust takes time to build, and it deepens through repetition. Each time you act in alignment with your values – even when it's hard – you reinforce it. Each time you speak up when you'd rather shrink back, or show compassion to yourself in failure, or choose growth over approval, you strengthen the trust you have in yourself.

The work you've done over the last nine days has helped you to understand your own confidence patterns, an increased awareness that will serve you well as you nurture your growing sense of humble confidence. Continue to notice your patterns: when does confidence show up easily? When does it slip away? Being aware of the triggers for both confidence and self-doubt helps you navigate what life throws at you with a greater degree of assurance and ease. Instead of being blindsided by a dip in self-belief, you can meet it with curiosity and compassion: *What's going on here? What do I need to remind myself of right now?*

Continuing to strengthen the muscle

Confidence is like a muscle – continuous use is what keeps it strong. Keep putting yourself in situations that stretch you, even just a little. Keep saying yes when you'd rather play it safe. Keep feeling the fear and doing it anyway. Each time you do, you reinforce the (true) story that you *can* figure things out – that you're capable, adaptable and growing.

And while we're talking about stories, I have one final thought to offer about the inner critic – that storyteller of doom who keeps up a commentary of self-doubt. Your inner critic will continue to accompany you as you build and sustain your confidence, but you are (I hope) now much better equipped to respond constructively to its input. Next time you notice this negative storyteller step up to the microphone, try countering this critical voice with a voice of compassion. Pause, take a breath and then ask yourself, 'if a friend were to find themselves in the situation that I'm in right now, what would I say to them?' It's a powerful in-the-moment tool to access some self-compassion.

So what? Over to you...

1. Take a moment to look back through your answers to all of the self-coaching questions for Days 1 to 9. What have you learned about your confidence patterns?

2. What's the next opportunity you have to 'feel the fear and do it anyway'? What – or who – will help you flex your confidence muscle and say 'yes'?

3. What's one commitment you'll make to yourself to keep growing your confidence from here?

Conclusion

You can find your confidence in the words that you choose and in the strength of your voice. You can find it in the opportunities and challenges that you embrace. You can find it in your thoughtful, curious response to setbacks. You can find it in the dialogue you have with your inner critic. Above all, you can find your confidence within yourself.

My intention over the past ten days has been to act as a guide, offering ideas and activities to help you to unearth – and to grow – your trust in yourself.

I hope that you now feel able to describe your confidence more fully, to understand its drivers, and to spot the moments when it falters. I hope that you've met your self-doubt with curiosity and compassion. I hope that you're already experimenting with ways to lean into your self-belief and to quieten your self-doubt. I hope that the confidence aspiration which you set out on Day 1 feels more attainable, that you're already seeing glimpses of the shifts that you imagined.

Find Your Confidence

You know that growing confidence takes time. In the coming weeks and months, remember to take a step back every so often to notice and appreciate the progress that you're making. Think about the ways in which you have already made small steps towards deeper self-trust. All of these small steps matter because over time they add up to significant growth.

I'm delighted that you've come this far and I know that you can continue to grow your confidence. I have every faith in you.

Endnotes

1 In *Untamed: Stop Pleasing, Start Living*. Vermilion. 2020.

2 In *The Inner Game of Tennis*. Pan Books. 1986.

3 Ian Robertson, *How Confidence Works: The New Science of Self-Belief*. Transworld Digital. Kindle Edition. 2021.

4 Referenced in Ian Stewart and Vann Joines, *TA Today: A New Introduction to Transactional Analysis*. Lifespace Publishing. 1987.

5 Cited in Sarah Lewis, *The Rise: Creativity, the Gift of Failure, and the Search for Mastery*. William Collins. 2015.

Enjoyed this?
Then you'll love...

Coach Yourself Confident by Julie Smith

WINNER getAbstract International Book Award 2024 – Business Impact, Readers' Choice

Business Book Awards 2025 Finalist

The People's Book Prize Longlisted Title 2024/25

'I devoured every page of this wonderfully written book.' – Sergio Ezama, Chief Talent Officer, Netflix

Want to be more confident at work? You're not alone.

So many of us grapple with self-doubt.

Perhaps you're an exhausted achiever? You're delivering results and progressing in your career, but you feel utterly worn out. You're compensating for a lack of confidence with excessive effort and punishingly high standards.

Or perhaps you're feeling frustrated and unfulfilled? Self-doubt is making you hold yourself back, you're avoiding challenges that could demonstrate how good you really are.

This book can help. Distilling over a decade of real-life research into clear insights, practical tools and impactful activities, Julie Smith shows you how to *Coach Yourself Confident*.

Other *6-Minute Smarts* titles

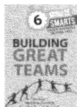
Building Great Teams (based on *Workshop Culture* by Alison Coward)

Collaborate Better (based on *Collabor(h)ate* by Deb Mashek PhD)

Customer Success Essentials (based on *The Customer Success Pioneer* by Kellie Lucas)

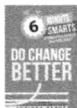
Do Change Better (based on *How to be a Change Superhero* by Lucinda Carney)

Get That Promotion (based on *Getting On* by Joanna Gaudoin)

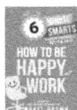
How to be Happy at Work (based on *My Job Isn't Working!* by Michael Brown)

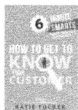

How to Get to Know Your Customer (based on *Do Penguins Eat Peaches?* by Katie Tucker)

The Listening Leader (based on *The Listening Shift* by Janie Van Hool)

Mastering People Management (based on *Mission: To Manage* by Marianne Page)

Managing Big Teams (based on *Big Teams* by Tony Llewellyn)

No-Nonsense PR (based on *Hype Yourself* by Lucy Werner)

Present Like a Pro (based on *Executive Presentations* by Jacqui Harper)

Reimagine Your Career (based on *Work/Life Flywheel* by Ollie Henderson)

Sales Made Simple (based on *More Sales Please* by Sara Nasser Dalrymple)

The Speed Storytelling Toolkit (based on *Exposure* by Felicity Cowie)

Stay Focused (based on *Attention!* by Rob Hatch)

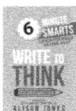

Write to Think (based on *Exploratory Writing* by Alison Jones)

Look out for more titles coming soon! Visit www.practicalinspiration.com for all our latest titles.

www.ingramcontent.com/pod-product-compliance
Lightning Source LLC
Chambersburg PA
CBHW020555030426
42337CB00013B/1104